The Survivors Journal Book
Book
Becoming A Warrior
Of Survival

Donna Taylor

DON'T BE ASHAMED OF YOUR SCARS
AND BATTLE WOUNDS THEY ARE
REMINDERS THAT YOU ARE A WARRIOR
OF SURVIVAL AND THAT YOU SURVIVED
YOUR DOMESTIC VIOLENCE JOURNEY

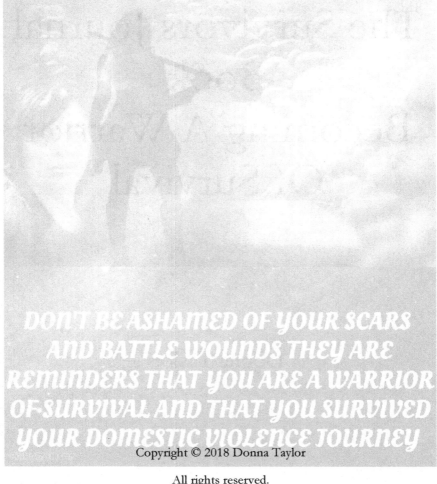

DON'T BE ASHAMED OF YOUR SCARS
AND BATTLE WOUNDS THEY ARE
REMINDERS THAT YOU ARE A WARRIOR
OF SURVIVAL AND THAT YOU SURVIVED
YOUR DOMESTIC VIOLENCE JOURNEY

ISBN:1727740645
ISBN-13:978-1727740646

DEDICATION

I would like to dedicate this book to all survivors of domestic violence.
Encouraging survivors to be able to one day share their domestic violence
journal with others while turning their tragedy of domestic violence into a
journey of inspiration, motivation, encouragment, and a journey filled with
blessings.

DON'T BE ASHAMED OF YOUR SCARS
AND BATTLE WOUNDS THEY ARE
REMINDERS THAT YOU ARE A WARRIOR
OF SURVIVAL AND THAT YOU SURVIVED
YOUR DOMESTIC VIOLENCE JOURNEY

DON'T BE ASHAMED OF YOUR SCARS
AND BATTLE WOUNDS THEY ARE
REMINDERS THAT YOU ARE A WARRIOR
OF SURVIVAL AND THAT YOU SURVIVED
YOUR DOMESTIC VIOLENCE JOURNEY

CONTENTS

DON'T BE ASHAMED OF YOUR SCARS
AND BATTLE WOUNDS THEY ARE
REMINDERS THAT YOU ARE A WARRIOR
OF SURVIVAL AND THAT YOU SURVIVED
YOUR DOMESTIC VIOLENCE JOURNEY

DON'T BE ASHAMED OF YOUR SCARS
AND BATTLE WOUNDS THEY ARE
REMINDERS THAT YOU ARE A WARRIOR
OF SURVIVAL AND THAT YOU SURVIVED
YOUR DOMESTIC VIOLENCE JOURNEY

ACKNOWLEDGMENTS

I would first like to give honor and glory to God for giving me the wisdom, knowledge, and understanding to be able to share my domestic violence journey and turn my journey into an organization that provides assistance to others. I would also like to acknowledge Sols Writing Center and Ms. Sherri Williams for the motivation, inspiration, and support which lead to the inspiration of following my dreams and acomplishing my goals.

DON'T BE ASHAMED OF YOUR SCARS AND BATTLE WOUNDS THEY ARE REMINDERS THAT YOU ARE A WARRIOR OF SURVIVAL AND THAT YOU SURVIVED YOUR DOMESTIC VIOLENCE JOURNEY

i

DON'T BE ASHAMED OF YOUR SCARS
AND BATTLE WOUNDS THEY ARE
REMINDERS THAT YOU ARE A WARRIOR
OF-SURVIVAL AND THAT YOU SURVIVED
YOUR DOMESTIC VIOLENCE JOURNEY

DON'T BE ASHAMED OF YOUR SCARS AND BATTLE WOUNDS THEY ARE REMINDERS THAT YOU ARE A WARRIOR OF SURVIVAL AND THAT YOU SURVIVED YOUR DOMESTIC VIOLENCE JOURNEY

DON'T BE ASHAMED OF YOUR SCARS AND BATTLE WOUNDS THEY ARE REMINDERS THAT YOU ARE A WARRIOR OF SURVIVAL AND THAT YOU SURVIVED YOUR DOMESTIC VIOLENCE JOURNEY

DON'T BE ASHAMED OF YOUR SCARS AND BATTLE WOUNDS THEY ARE REMINDERS THAT YOU ARE A WARRIOR OF SURVIVAL AND THAT YOU SURVIVED YOUR DOMESTIC VIOLENCE JOURNEY

DON'T BE ASHAMED OF YOUR SCARS AND BATTLE WOUNDS THEY ARE REMINDERS THAT YOU ARE A WARRIOR OF SURVIVAL AND THAT YOU SURVIVED YOUR DOMESTIC VIOLENCE JOURNEY

4

DON'T BE ASHAMED OF YOUR SCARS
AND BATTLE WOUNDS THEY ARE
REMINDERS THAT YOU ARE A WARRIOR
OF SURVIVAL AND THAT YOU SURVIVED
YOUR DOMESTIC VIOLENCE JOURNEY

DON'T BE ASHAMED OF YOUR SCARS AND BATTLE WOUNDS THEY ARE REMINDERS THAT YOU ARE A WARRIOR OF SURVIVAL AND THAT YOU SURVIVED YOUR DOMESTIC VIOLENCE JOURNEY

_____

_____

_____

_____

_____

_____

_____

_____

_____

_____

_____

_____

_____

DON'T BE ASHAMED OF YOUR SCARS
AND BATTLE WOUNDS THEY ARE
REMINDERS THAT YOU ARE A WARRIOR
OF SURVIVAL AND THAT YOU SURVIVED
YOUR DOMESTIC VIOLENCE JOURNEY

_____

_____

DON'T BE ASHAMED OF YOUR SCARS AND BATTLE WOUNDS THEY ARE REMINDERS THAT YOU ARE A WARRIOR OF SURVIVAL AND THAT YOU SURVIVED YOUR DOMESTIC VIOLENCE JOURNEY

DON'T BE ASHAMED OF YOUR SCARS AND BATTLE WOUNDS THEY ARE REMINDERS THAT YOU ARE A WARRIOR OF SURVIVAL AND THAT YOU SURVIVED YOUR DOMESTIC VIOLENCE JOURNEY

DON'T BE ASHAMED OF YOUR SCARS AND BATTLE WOUNDS THEY ARE REMINDERS THAT YOU ARE A WARRIOR OF SURVIVAL AND THAT YOU SURVIVED YOUR DOMESTIC VIOLENCE JOURNEY

DON'T BE ASHAMED OF YOUR SCARS AND BATTLE WOUNDS THEY ARE REMINDERS THAT YOU ARE A WARRIOR OF SURVIVAL AND THAT YOU SURVIVED YOUR DOMESTIC VIOLENCE JOURNEY

DON'T BE ASHAMED OF YOUR SCARS AND BATTLE WOUNDS THEY ARE REMINDERS THAT YOU ARE A WARRIOR OF SURVIVAL AND THAT YOU SURVIVED YOUR DOMESTIC VIOLENCE JOURNEY

_____

_____

_____

_____

_____

_____

_____

_____

_____

_____

_____

_____

_____

_____

_____

_____

_____

DON'T BE ASHAMED OF YOUR SCARS
AND BATTLE WOUNDS THEY ARE
REMINDERS THAT YOU ARE A WARRIOR
OF SURVIVAL AND THAT YOU SURVIVED
YOUR DOMESTIC VIOLENCE JOURNEY

_____

_____

DON'T BE ASHAMED OF YOUR SCARS
AND BATTLE WOUNDS THEY ARE
REMINDERS THAT YOU ARE A WARRIOR
OF SURVIVAL AND THAT YOU SURVIVED
YOUR DOMESTIC VIOLENCE JOURNEY

DON'T BE ASHAMED OF YOUR SCARS AND BATTLE WOUNDS THEY ARE REMINDERS THAT YOU ARE A WARRIOR OF SURVIVAL AND THAT YOU SURVIVED YOUR DOMESTIC VIOLENCE JOURNEY

DON'T BE ASHAMED OF YOUR SCARS AND BATTLE WOUNDS THEY ARE REMINDERS THAT YOU ARE A WARRIOR OF SURVIVAL AND THAT YOU SURVIVED YOUR DOMESTIC VIOLENCE JOURNEY

DON'T BE ASHAMED OF YOUR SCARS AND BATTLE WOUNDS THEY ARE REMINDERS THAT YOU ARE A WARRIOR OF SURVIVAL AND THAT YOU SURVIVED YOUR DOMESTIC VIOLENCE JOURNEY

DON'T BE ASHAMED OF YOUR SCARS
AND BATTLE WOUNDS THEY ARE
REMINDERS THAT YOU ARE A WARRIOR
OF SURVIVAL AND THAT YOU SURVIVED
YOUR DOMESTIC VIOLENCE JOURNEY

DON'T BE ASHAMED OF YOUR SCARS AND BATTLE WOUNDS THEY ARE REMINDERS THAT YOU ARE A WARRIOR OF SURVIVAL AND THAT YOU SURVIVED YOUR DOMESTIC VIOLENCE JOURNEY

DON'T BE ASHAMED OF YOUR SCARS AND BATTLE WOUNDS THEY ARE REMINDERS THAT YOU ARE A WARRIOR OF SURVIVAL AND THAT YOU SURVIVED YOUR DOMESTIC VIOLENCE JOURNEY

_____

_____

_____

_____

_____

_____

_____

_____

_____

_____

_____

_____

_____

_____

DON'T BE ASHAMED OF YOUR SCARS
AND BATTLE WOUNDS THEY ARE
REMINDERS THAT YOU ARE A WARRIOR
OF SURVIVAL AND THAT YOU SURVIVED
YOUR DOMESTIC VIOLENCE JOURNEY

_____

_____

DON'T BE ASHAMED OF YOUR SCARS AND BATTLE WOUNDS THEY ARE REMINDERS THAT YOU ARE A WARRIOR OF SURVIVAL AND THAT YOU SURVIVED YOUR DOMESTIC VIOLENCE JOURNEY

DON'T BE ASHAMED OF YOUR SCARS
AND BATTLE WOUNDS THEY ARE
REMINDERS THAT YOU ARE A WARRIOR
OF SURVIVAL AND THAT YOU SURVIVED
YOUR DOMESTIC VIOLENCE JOURNEY

DON'T BE ASHAMED OF YOUR SCARS AND BATTLE WOUNDS THEY ARE REMINDERS THAT YOU ARE A WARRIOR OF SURVIVAL AND THAT YOU SURVIVED YOUR DOMESTIC VIOLENCE JOURNEY

DON'T BE ASHAMED OF YOUR SCARS AND BATTLE WOUNDS THEY ARE REMINDERS THAT YOU ARE A WARRIOR OF SURVIVAL AND THAT YOU SURVIVED YOUR DOMESTIC VIOLENCE JOURNEY

DON'T BE ASHAMED OF YOUR SCARS
AND BATTLE WOUNDS THEY ARE
REMINDERS THAT YOU ARE A WARRIOR
OF SURVIVAL AND THAT YOU SURVIVED
YOUR DOMESTIC VIOLENCE JOURNEY

DON'T BE ASHAMED OF YOUR SCARS AND BATTLE WOUNDS THEY ARE REMINDERS THAT YOU ARE A WARRIOR OF SURVIVAL AND THAT YOU SURVIVED YOUR DOMESTIC VIOLENCE JOURNEY

DON'T BE ASHAMED OF YOUR SCARS
AND BATTLE WOUNDS THEY ARE
REMINDERS THAT YOU ARE A WARRIOR
OF SURVIVAL AND THAT YOU SURVIVED
YOUR DOMESTIC VIOLENCE JOURNEY

DON'T BE ASHAMED OF YOUR SCARS AND BATTLE WOUNDS THEY ARE REMINDERS THAT YOU ARE A WARRIOR OF SURVIVAL AND THAT YOU SURVIVED YOUR DOMESTIC VIOLENCE JOURNEY

DON'T BE ASHAMED OF YOUR SCARS AND BATTLE WOUNDS THEY ARE REMINDERS THAT YOU ARE A WARRIOR OF SURVIVAL AND THAT YOU SURVIVED YOUR DOMESTIC VIOLENCE JOURNEY

DON'T BE ASHAMED OF YOUR SCARS
AND BATTLE WOUNDS THEY ARE
REMINDERS THAT YOU ARE A WARRIOR
OF SURVIVAL AND THAT YOU SURVIVED
YOUR DOMESTIC VIOLENCE JOURNEY

DON'T BE ASHAMED OF YOUR SCARS
AND BATTLE WOUNDS THEY ARE
REMINDERS THAT YOU ARE A WARRIOR
OF SURVIVAL AND THAT YOU SURVIVED
YOUR DOMESTIC VIOLENCE JOURNEY

_____

_____

_____

_____

_____

_____

_____

_____

_____

_____

_____

_____

_____

DON'T BE ASHAMED OF YOUR SCARS
AND BATTLE WOUNDS THEY ARE
REMINDERS THAT YOU ARE A WARRIOR
OF SURVIVAL AND THAT YOU SURVIVED
YOUR DOMESTIC VIOLENCE JOURNEY

_____

_____

DON'T BE ASHAMED OF YOUR SCARS AND BATTLE WOUNDS THEY ARE REMINDERS THAT YOU ARE A WARRIOR OF SURVIVAL AND THAT YOU SURVIVED YOUR DOMESTIC VIOLENCE JOURNEY

DON'T BE ASHAMED OF YOUR SCARS AND BATTLE WOUNDS THEY ARE REMINDERS THAT YOU ARE A WARRIOR OF SURVIVAL AND THAT YOU SURVIVED YOUR DOMESTIC VIOLENCE JOURNEY

DON'T BE ASHAMED OF YOUR SCARS
AND BATTLE WOUNDS THEY ARE
REMINDERS THAT YOU ARE A WARRIOR
OF SURVIVAL AND THAT YOU SURVIVED
YOUR DOMESTIC VIOLENCE JOURNEY

_____

_____

_____

_____

_____

_____

_____

_____

_____

_____

_____

_____

_____

_____

_____

_____

DON'T BE ASHAMED OF YOUR SCARS
AND BATTLE WOUNDS THEY ARE
REMINDERS THAT YOU ARE A WARRIOR
OF SURVIVAL AND THAT YOU SURVIVED
YOUR DOMESTIC VIOLENCE JOURNEY

_____

_____

DON'T BE ASHAMED OF YOUR SCARS AND BATTLE WOUNDS THEY ARE REMINDERS THAT YOU ARE A WARRIOR OF SURVIVAL AND THAT YOU SURVIVED YOUR DOMESTIC VIOLENCE JOURNEY

DON'T BE ASHAMED OF YOUR SCARS AND BATTLE WOUNDS THEY ARE REMINDERS THAT YOU ARE A WARRIOR OF SURVIVAL AND THAT YOU SURVIVED YOUR DOMESTIC VIOLENCE JOURNEY

DON'T BE ASHAMED OF YOUR SCARS
AND BATTLE WOUNDS THEY ARE
REMINDERS THAT YOU ARE A WARRIOR
OF SURVIVAL AND THAT YOU SURVIVED
YOUR DOMESTIC VIOLENCE JOURNEY

DON'T BE ASHAMED OF YOUR SCARS
AND BATTLE WOUNDS THEY ARE
REMINDERS THAT YOU ARE A WARRIOR
OF SURVIVAL AND THAT YOU SURVIVED
YOUR DOMESTIC VIOLENCE JOURNEY

DON'T BE ASHAMED OF YOUR SCARS AND BATTLE WOUNDS THEY ARE REMINDERS THAT YOU ARE A WARRIOR OF SURVIVAL AND THAT YOU SURVIVED YOUR DOMESTIC VIOLENCE JOURNEY

DON'T BE ASHAMED OF YOUR SCARS AND BATTLE WOUNDS THEY ARE REMINDERS THAT YOU ARE A WARRIOR OF SURVIVAL AND THAT YOU SURVIVED YOUR DOMESTIC VIOLENCE JOURNEY

DON'T BE ASHAMED OF YOUR SCARS
AND BATTLE WOUNDS THEY ARE
REMINDERS THAT YOU ARE A WARRIOR
OF SURVIVAL AND THAT YOU SURVIVED
YOUR DOMESTIC VIOLENCE JOURNEY

DON'T BE ASHAMED OF YOUR SCARS
AND BATTLE WOUNDS THEY ARE
REMINDERS THAT YOU ARE A WARRIOR
OF SURVIVAL AND THAT YOU SURVIVED
YOUR DOMESTIC VIOLENCE JOURNEY

DON'T BE ASHAMED OF YOUR SCARS AND BATTLE WOUNDS THEY ARE REMINDERS THAT YOU ARE A WARRIOR OF SURVIVAL AND THAT YOU SURVIVED YOUR DOMESTIC VIOLENCE JOURNEY

DON'T BE ASHAMED OF YOUR SCARS AND BATTLE WOUNDS THEY ARE REMINDERS THAT YOU ARE A WARRIOR OF SURVIVAL AND THAT YOU SURVIVED YOUR DOMESTIC VIOLENCE JOURNEY

DON'T BE ASHAMED OF YOUR SCARS AND BATTLE WOUNDS THEY ARE REMINDERS THAT YOU ARE A WARRIOR OF SURVIVAL AND THAT YOU SURVIVED YOUR DOMESTIC VIOLENCE JOURNEY

DON'T BE ASHAMED OF YOUR SCARS AND BATTLE WOUNDS THEY ARE REMINDERS THAT YOU ARE A WARRIOR OF SURVIVAL AND THAT YOU SURVIVED YOUR DOMESTIC VIOLENCE JOURNEY

DON'T BE ASHAMED OF YOUR SCARS AND BATTLE WOUNDS THEY ARE REMINDERS THAT YOU ARE A WARRIOR OF SURVIVAL AND THAT YOU SURVIVED YOUR DOMESTIC VIOLENCE JOURNEY

DON'T BE ASHAMED OF YOUR SCARS
AND BATTLE WOUNDS THEY ARE
REMINDERS THAT YOU ARE A WARRIOR
OF SURVIVAL AND THAT YOU SURVIVED
YOUR DOMESTIC VIOLENCE JOURNEY

DON'T BE ASHAMED OF YOUR SCARS AND BATTLE WOUNDS THEY ARE REMINDERS THAT YOU ARE A WARRIOR OF SURVIVAL AND THAT YOU SURVIVED YOUR DOMESTIC VIOLENCE JOURNEY

_____

_____

_____

_____

_____

_____

_____

_____

_____

_____

_____

_____

_____

DON'T BE ASHAMED OF YOUR SCARS
AND BATTLE WOUNDS THEY ARE
REMINDERS THAT YOU ARE A WARRIOR
OF SURVIVAL AND THAT YOU SURVIVED
YOUR DOMESTIC VIOLENCE JOURNEY

_____

_____

DON'T BE ASHAMED OF YOUR SCARS AND BATTLE WOUNDS THEY ARE REMINDERS THAT YOU ARE A WARRIOR OF SURVIVAL AND THAT YOU SURVIVED YOUR DOMESTIC VIOLENCE JOURNEY

DON'T BE ASHAMED OF YOUR SCARS AND BATTLE WOUNDS THEY ARE REMINDERS THAT YOU ARE A WARRIOR OF SURVIVAL AND THAT YOU SURVIVED YOUR DOMESTIC VIOLENCE JOURNEY

DON'T BE ASHAMED OF YOUR SCARS
AND BATTLE WOUNDS THEY ARE
REMINDERS THAT YOU ARE A WARRIOR
OF SURVIVAL AND THAT YOU SURVIVED
YOUR DOMESTIC VIOLENCE JOURNEY

DON'T BE ASHAMED OF YOUR SCARS AND BATTLE WOUNDS THEY ARE REMINDERS THAT YOU ARE A WARRIOR OF SURVIVAL AND THAT YOU SURVIVED YOUR DOMESTIC VIOLENCE JOURNEY

DON'T BE ASHAMED OF YOUR SCARS
AND BATTLE WOUNDS THEY ARE
REMINDERS THAT YOU ARE A WARRIOR
OF SURVIVAL AND THAT YOU SURVIVED
YOUR DOMESTIC VIOLENCE JOURNEY

DON'T BE ASHAMED OF YOUR SCARS
AND BATTLE WOUNDS THEY ARE
REMINDERS THAT YOU ARE A WARRIOR
OF SURVIVAL AND THAT YOU SURVIVED
YOUR DOMESTIC VIOLENCE JOURNEY

DON'T BE ASHAMED OF YOUR SCARS
AND BATTLE WOUNDS THEY ARE
REMINDERS THAT YOU ARE A WARRIOR
OF SURVIVAL AND THAT YOU SURVIVED
YOUR DOMESTIC VIOLENCE JOURNEY

DON'T BE ASHAMED OF YOUR SCARS
AND BATTLE WOUNDS THEY ARE
REMINDERS THAT YOU ARE A WARRIOR
OF SURVIVAL AND THAT YOU SURVIVED
YOUR DOMESTIC VIOLENCE JOURNEY

DON'T BE ASHAMED OF YOUR SCARS AND BATTLE WOUNDS THEY ARE REMINDERS THAT YOU ARE A WARRIOR OF SURVIVAL AND THAT YOU SURVIVED YOUR DOMESTIC VIOLENCE JOURNEY

DON'T BE ASHAMED OF YOUR SCARS
AND BATTLE WOUNDS THEY ARE
REMINDERS THAT YOU ARE A WARRIOR
OF SURVIVAL AND THAT YOU SURVIVED
YOUR DOMESTIC VIOLENCE JOURNEY

DON'T BE ASHAMED OF YOUR SCARS
AND BATTLE WOUNDS THEY ARE
REMINDERS THAT YOU ARE A WARRIOR
OF SURVIVAL AND THAT YOU SURVIVED
YOUR DOMESTIC VIOLENCE JOURNEY

DON'T BE ASHAMED OF YOUR SCARS
AND BATTLE WOUNDS THEY ARE
REMINDERS THAT YOU ARE A WARRIOR
OF SURVIVAL AND THAT YOU SURVIVED
YOUR DOMESTIC VIOLENCE JOURNEY

DON'T BE ASHAMED OF YOUR SCARS AND BATTLE WOUNDS THEY ARE REMINDERS THAT YOU ARE A WARRIOR OF SURVIVAL AND THAT YOU SURVIVED YOUR DOMESTIC VIOLENCE JOURNEY

DON'T BE ASHAMED OF YOUR SCARS
AND BATTLE WOUNDS THEY ARE
REMINDERS THAT YOU ARE A WARRIOR
OF SURVIVAL AND THAT YOU SURVIVED
YOUR DOMESTIC VIOLENCE JOURNEY

DON'T BE ASHAMED OF YOUR SCARS AND BATTLE WOUNDS THEY ARE REMINDERS THAT YOU ARE A WARRIOR OF SURVIVAL AND THAT YOU SURVIVED YOUR DOMESTIC VIOLENCE JOURNEY

DON'T BE ASHAMED OF YOUR SCARS
AND BATTLE WOUNDS THEY ARE
REMINDERS THAT YOU ARE A WARRIOR
OF SURVIVAL AND THAT YOU SURVIVED
YOUR DOMESTIC VIOLENCE JOURNEY

DON'T BE ASHAMED OF YOUR SCARS AND BATTLE WOUNDS THEY ARE REMINDERS THAT YOU ARE A WARRIOR OF SURVIVAL AND THAT YOU SURVIVED YOUR DOMESTIC VIOLENCE JOURNEY

DON'T BE ASHAMED OF YOUR SCARS AND BATTLE WOUNDS THEY ARE REMINDERS THAT YOU ARE A WARRIOR OF SURVIVAL AND THAT YOU SURVIVED YOUR DOMESTIC VIOLENCE JOURNEY

DON'T BE ASHAMED OF YOUR SCARS
AND BATTLE WOUNDS THEY ARE
REMINDERS THAT YOU ARE A WARRIOR
OF SURVIVAL AND THAT YOU SURVIVED
YOUR DOMESTIC VIOLENCE JOURNEY

DON'T BE ASHAMED OF YOUR SCARS AND BATTLE WOUNDS THEY ARE REMINDERS THAT YOU ARE A WARRIOR OF SURVIVAL AND THAT YOU SURVIVED YOUR DOMESTIC VIOLENCE JOURNEY

DON'T BE ASHAMED OF YOUR SCARS AND BATTLE WOUNDS THEY ARE REMINDERS THAT YOU ARE A WARRIOR OF SURVIVAL AND THAT YOU SURVIVED YOUR DOMESTIC VIOLENCE JOURNEY

DON'T BE ASHAMED OF YOUR SCARS AND BATTLE WOUNDS THEY ARE REMINDERS THAT YOU ARE A WARRIOR OF SURVIVAL AND THAT YOU SURVIVED YOUR DOMESTIC VIOLENCE JOURNEY

DON'T BE ASHAMED OF YOUR SCARS
AND BATTLE WOUNDS THEY ARE
REMINDERS THAT YOU ARE A WARRIOR
OF SURVIVAL AND THAT YOU SURVIVED
YOUR DOMESTIC VIOLENCE JOURNEY

DON'T BE ASHAMED OF YOUR SCARS AND BATTLE WOUNDS THEY ARE REMINDERS THAT YOU ARE A WARRIOR OF SURVIVAL AND THAT YOU SURVIVED YOUR DOMESTIC VIOLENCE JOURNEY

DON'T BE ASHAMED OF YOUR SCARS
AND BATTLE WOUNDS THEY ARE
REMINDERS THAT YOU ARE A WARRIOR
OF SURVIVAL AND THAT YOU SURVIVED
YOUR DOMESTIC VIOLENCE JOURNEY

DON'T BE ASHAMED OF YOUR SCARS AND BATTLE WOUNDS THEY ARE REMINDERS THAT YOU ARE A WARRIOR OF SURVIVAL AND THAT YOU SURVIVED YOUR DOMESTIC VIOLENCE JOURNEY

DON'T BE ASHAMED OF YOUR SCARS
AND BATTLE WOUNDS THEY ARE
REMINDERS THAT YOU ARE A WARRIOR
OF SURVIVAL AND THAT YOU SURVIVED
YOUR DOMESTIC VIOLENCE JOURNEY

DON'T BE ASHAMED OF YOUR SCARS AND BATTLE WOUNDS THEY ARE REMINDERS THAT YOU ARE A WARRIOR OF SURVIVAL AND THAT YOU SURVIVED YOUR DOMESTIC VIOLENCE JOURNEY

DON'T BE ASHAMED OF YOUR SCARS AND BATTLE WOUNDS THEY ARE REMINDERS THAT YOU ARE A WARRIOR OF SURVIVAL AND THAT YOU SURVIVED YOUR DOMESTIC VIOLENCE JOURNEY

DON'T BE ASHAMED OF YOUR SCARS
AND BATTLE WOUNDS THEY ARE
REMINDERS THAT YOU ARE A WARRIOR
OF SURVIVAL AND THAT YOU SURVIVED
YOUR DOMESTIC VIOLENCE JOURNEY

DON'T BE ASHAMED OF YOUR SCARS AND BATTLE WOUNDS THEY ARE REMINDERS THAT YOU ARE A WARRIOR OF SURVIVAL AND THAT YOU SURVIVED YOUR DOMESTIC VIOLENCE JOURNEY

DON'T BE ASHAMED OF YOUR SCARS AND BATTLE WOUNDS THEY ARE REMINDERS THAT YOU ARE A WARRIOR OF SURVIVAL AND THAT YOU SURVIVED YOUR DOMESTIC VIOLENCE JOURNEY

DON'T BE ASHAMED OF YOUR SCARS AND BATTLE WOUNDS THEY ARE REMINDERS THAT YOU ARE A WARRIOR OF SURVIVAL AND THAT YOU SURVIVED YOUR DOMESTIC VIOLENCE JOURNEY

DON'T BE ASHAMED OF YOUR SCARS AND BATTLE WOUNDS THEY ARE REMINDERS THAT YOU ARE A WARRIOR OF SURVIVAL AND THAT YOU SURVIVED YOUR DOMESTIC VIOLENCE JOURNEY

DON'T BE ASHAMED OF YOUR SCARS AND BATTLE WOUNDS THEY ARE REMINDERS THAT YOU ARE A WARRIOR OF SURVIVAL AND THAT YOU SURVIVED YOUR DOMESTIC VIOLENCE JOURNEY

DON'T BE ASHAMED OF YOUR SCARS
AND BATTLE WOUNDS THEY ARE
REMINDERS THAT YOU ARE A WARRIOR
OF SURVIVAL AND THAT YOU SURVIVED
YOUR DOMESTIC VIOLENCE JOURNEY

DON'T BE ASHAMED OF YOUR SCARS
AND BATTLE WOUNDS THEY ARE
REMINDERS THAT YOU ARE A WARRIOR
OF SURVIVAL AND THAT YOU SURVIVED
YOUR DOMESTIC VIOLENCE JOURNEY

DON'T BE ASHAMED OF YOUR SCARS AND BATTLE WOUNDS THEY ARE REMINDERS THAT YOU ARE A WARRIOR OF SURVIVAL AND THAT YOU SURVIVED YOUR DOMESTIC VIOLENCE JOURNEY

DON'T BE ASHAMED OF YOUR SCARS AND BATTLE WOUNDS THEY ARE REMINDERS THAT YOU ARE A WARRIOR OF SURVIVAL AND THAT YOU SURVIVED YOUR DOMESTIC VIOLENCE JOURNEY

DON'T BE ASHAMED OF YOUR SCARS
AND BATTLE WOUNDS THEY ARE
REMINDERS THAT YOU ARE A WARRIOR
OF SURVIVAL AND THAT YOU SURVIVED
YOUR DOMESTIC VIOLENCE JOURNEY

DON'T BE ASHAMED OF YOUR SCARS AND BATTLE WOUNDS THEY ARE REMINDERS THAT YOU ARE A WARRIOR OF SURVIVAL AND THAT YOU SURVIVED YOUR DOMESTIC VIOLENCE JOURNEY

DON'T BE ASHAMED OF YOUR SCARS AND BATTLE WOUNDS THEY ARE REMINDERS THAT YOU ARE A WARRIOR OF SURVIVAL AND THAT YOU SURVIVED YOUR DOMESTIC VIOLENCE JOURNEY

DON'T BE ASHAMED OF YOUR SCARS
AND BATTLE WOUNDS THEY ARE
REMINDERS THAT YOU ARE A WARRIOR
OF SURVIVAL AND THAT YOU SURVIVED
YOUR DOMESTIC VIOLENCE JOURNEY

DON'T BE ASHAMED OF YOUR SCARS AND BATTLE WOUNDS THEY ARE REMINDERS THAT YOU ARE A WARRIOR OF SURVIVAL AND THAT YOU SURVIVED YOUR DOMESTIC VIOLENCE JOURNEY

DON'T BE ASHAMED OF YOUR SCARS
AND BATTLE WOUNDS THEY ARE
REMINDERS THAT YOU ARE A WARRIOR
OF SURVIVAL AND THAT YOU SURVIVED
YOUR DOMESTIC VIOLENCE JOURNEY

DON'T BE ASHAMED OF YOUR SCARS AND BATTLE WOUNDS THEY ARE REMINDERS THAT YOU ARE A WARRIOR OF SURVIVAL AND THAT YOU SURVIVED YOUR DOMESTIC VIOLENCE JOURNEY

DON'T BE ASHAMED OF YOUR SCARS AND BATTLE WOUNDS THEY ARE REMINDERS THAT YOU ARE A WARRIOR OF SURVIVAL AND THAT YOU SURVIVED YOUR DOMESTIC VIOLENCE JOURNEY

Entering into a journey of domestic violence can be very difficult for anyone to endure. The most important thing we must remember is how to survive through every trial and tribulation which in turn builds us stronger, as well as gives us wisdom, knowledge, and understanding. As well as going through trials and tribulations makes us who we become in the future. By taking Gods hand and letting him take over our devastating journey is the first step to becoming a warrior of survival. By taking Gods hand and letting him lead us out of our domestic violence journey will lead us into a journey that is filled with happiness, joy, and many blessings.

DON'T BE ASHAMED OF YOUR SCARS
AND BATTLE WOUNDS THEY ARE
REMINDERS THAT YOU ARE A WARRIOR
OF SURVIVAL AND THAT YOU SURVIVED
YOUR DOMESTIC VIOLENCE JOURNEY

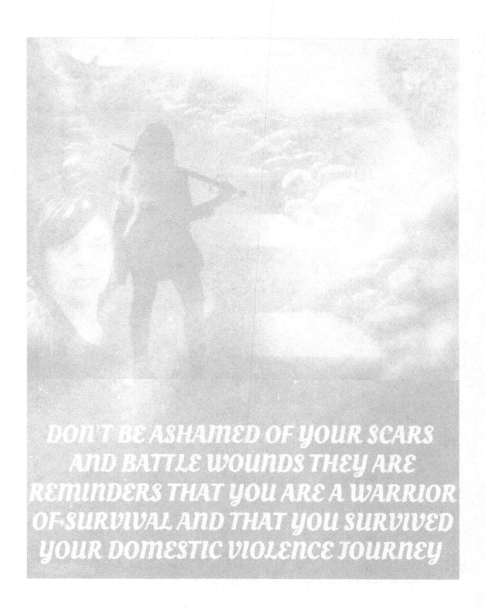

DON'T BE ASHAMED OF YOUR SCARS
AND BATTLE WOUNDS THEY ARE
REMINDERS THAT YOU ARE A WARRIOR
OF SURVIVAL AND THAT YOU SURVIVED
YOUR DOMESTIC VIOLENCE JOURNEY

DON'T BE ASHAMED OF YOUR SCARS
AND BATTLE WOUNDS THEY ARE
REMINDERS THAT YOU ARE A WARRIOR
OF SURVIVAL AND THAT YOU SURVIVED
YOUR DOMESTIC VIOLENCE JOURNEY

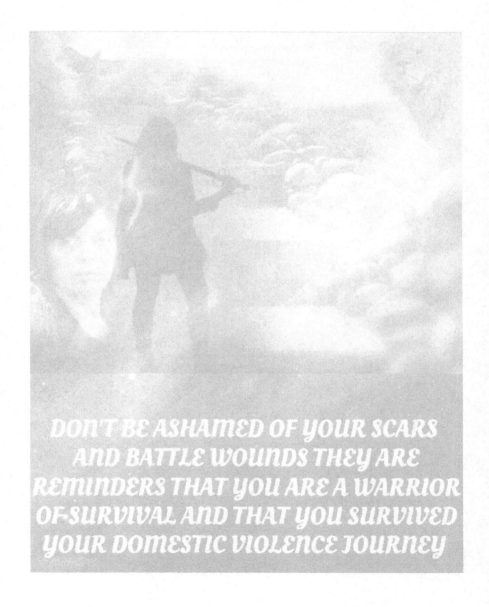

DON'T BE ASHAMED OF YOUR SCARS
AND BATTLE WOUNDS THEY ARE
REMINDERS THAT YOU ARE A WARRIOR
OF SURVIVAL AND THAT YOU SURVIVED
YOUR DOMESTIC VIOLENCE JOURNEY

DON'T BE ASHAMED OF YOUR SCARS
AND BATTLE WOUNDS THEY ARE
REMINDERS THAT YOU ARE A WARRIOR
OF SURVIVAL AND THAT YOU SURVIVED
YOUR DOMESTIC VIOLENCE JOURNEY

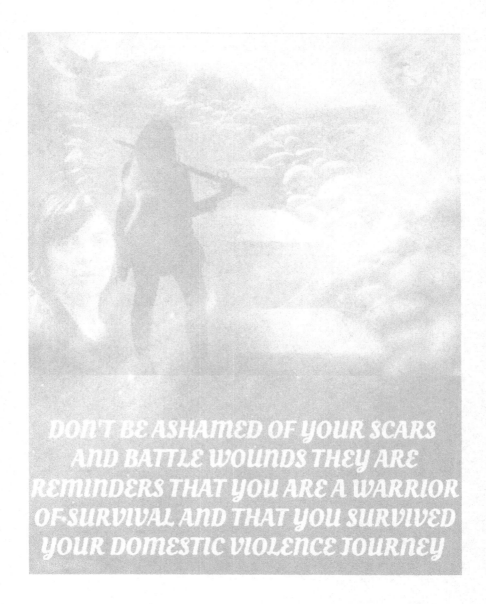

DON'T BE ASHAMED OF YOUR SCARS
AND BATTLE WOUNDS THEY ARE
REMINDERS THAT YOU ARE A WARRIOR
OF SURVIVAL AND THAT YOU SURVIVED
YOUR DOMESTIC VIOLENCE JOURNEY

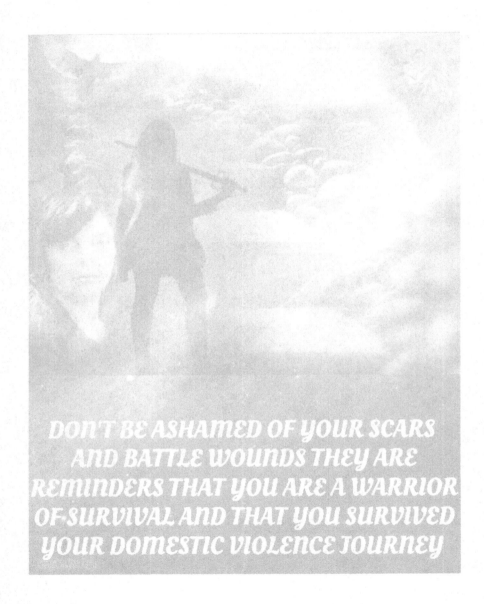

DON'T BE ASHAMED OF YOUR SCARS
AND BATTLE WOUNDS THEY ARE
REMINDERS THAT YOU ARE A WARRIOR
OF SURVIVAL AND THAT YOU SURVIVED
YOUR DOMESTIC VIOLENCE JOURNEY

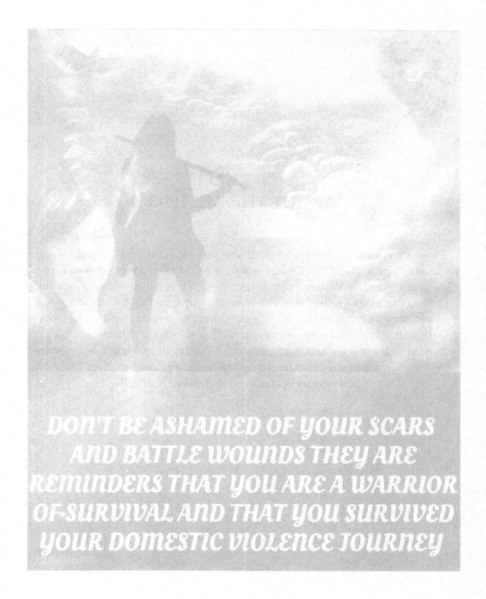

DON'T BE ASHAMED OF YOUR SCARS
AND BATTLE WOUNDS THEY ARE
REMINDERS THAT YOU ARE A WARRIOR
OF-SURVIVAL AND THAT YOU SURVIVED
YOUR DOMESTIC VIOLENCE JOURNEY

ABOUT THE AUTHOR

Donna Taylor is a survivor of domestic violence and is also a publishing author in Knoxville, TN. Donna is also the CEO/Founder of Warriors of Survival Domestic Violence Organization which is based out of Knoxville, TN. Donna published the The Survivors Journal Book Becoming A Warrior of Survival to be able to help others to one day be able to share their domestic violence journey, as well as to inspire others to not be ashamed of their scars and battle wounds of domestic violence because they are reminders that they survived their domestic violence journey and is on their way to becoming a warrior of survival.

DON'T BE ASHAMED OF YOUR SCARS AND BATTLE WOUNDS THEY ARE REMINDERS THAT YOU ARE A WARRIOR OF SURVIVAL AND THAT YOU SURVIVED YOUR DOMESTIC VIOLENCE JOURNEY

Made in the USA
Middletown, DE
04 August 2022

70606421R00066